Conversations

from

The Book of Matthew

A Devotional

Dr. Barbara Darby

Copyright 2025
ISBN: 979-8-9991700-8-8

Printed in the USA

edication

This Devotional is dedicated to my mother, Bethy Wanica Anderson, my maternal Grandmother, May Adelita Stephens, and the Fairclough and Barnaby families.

2 Timothy 1:5 - "I am reminded of your sincere faith, which first lived in your grandmother Lois and in your mother Eunice and, I am persuaded, now lives in you also," is a scripture that resonates in my heart, with different names. My faith journey began with my birth into maternal and paternal families who were believers in Jesus Christ. I was raised in the admonition of the Lord by both sides of the family and observed their practice of the Christian faith firsthand throughout my life.

But, it was my mother, Bethy Wanica, and my maternal grandmother, May Adelita, who had the greatest influence and most indelible impact, under the guidance of the Holy Spirit! While I joined the Presbyterian denomination when I relocated to Jacksonville, Florida. I was raised in the Catholic tradition and transitioned through the various phases of learning. These included Infant Baptism, Catechism classes, Confirmation, First Communion, Confession, attending Mass, and more.

As a young child, I was aware that the adults in my family practiced the Christian faith, held membership in churches of their choice, and participated in the life of their church. For example, my grandmother May played the organ for her church. I witnessed the two major influencers in my life pray in good and difficult times, pray for me and my safety and success in life continually, pray for friends and family members, visit the sick, and give to needy neighbors from the little they possessed. They lived out their faith as best they could and passed it on to me. It was the best gift they could have given me, and I am deeply grateful. I, in turn, have passed it on to my daughter, Tamara. Parents have a tremendous responsibility to raise their children in the admonition of the Lord, as they equip them for life in other ways.

Dr. Barbara Darby

reface

The Gospel of Matthew was written by a Jewish tax collector named Matthew who became one of Jesus' disciples. This Gospel connects the Old and New Testament because of its emphasis on the fulfillment of prophecy. Matthew wrote this Gospel to prove that JESUS is the Messiah, the eternal King.

For us as readers of this gospel, it is important to understand and keep in the forefront of our minds that Jesus is the Messiah and our Savior. Paul tells us in Romans 10:17, **"So then faith comes by hearing, and hearing by the word of God."** (**NKJV**) There is no better way to keep Jesus on our minds and to grow our faith than to have a daily devotion in the Word of God.

This devotional *"Conversations with GOD from the book of Matthew"* will allow you to connect with Jesus, share your thoughts, and to praise GOD as you reflect on Scripture from each chapter of the Gospel of Matthew.

It is important that we connect with Jesus. H tells us in John 15:5 **"Yes, I am the vine; you are the branches. Those who remain in me, and I in them, will produce much fruit. For apart from me you can do nothing".** (**NLT**)

I praise God for Dr. Barbara Darby allowing God to use her walk with the Lord to share with others, and I pray that reading these devotions will bring clarity to your journey with the Lord, and will encourage someone to accept The Lord Jesus as their personal Savior. John 3:3 **JESUS answered and said to him, "Most assuredly, I say to you, unless one is born again, he cannot see the Kingdom of GOD."**

Peace and Blessings
Rev. Don Johnson

*G*etting the most from this Devotional

Invite the Holy Spirit of God into your time of meditation and reflection. He will surely be present, guiding you as you open your heart to Him and listen for His still small voice.

Set aside time during each day and a quiet place to first read the entire chapter listed for each devotion. Reflect on the content of the scripture and what it says to you personally. Read the titled affirmation that follows and ask – Does it resonate in my heart? Is God speaking to me? What is He telling me?

Follow with penning your personal affirmation, lesson learned and expression of gratitude elicited by the day's devotion. Take action where the Spirit leads you. Once you have a collection of these personal affirmations, I encourage you to read what you have written a week, month, one or 5 years before and you will be blessed by what the Holy Spirit will reveal to you.

I began this practice in 1993 and have been richly blessed in my faith walk. And while I have at times not been consistent in my daily practice, I know that I am missing something very important – my conversations with God- and I get right back on track. So, just keep working at it, and the Lord will bring you to where He wants you to be in your spiritual growth.

Blessings,

Dr. Barbara Darby

Chapter 1

Verse to Remember: 1

> *This is the genealogy of Jesus the Messiah, the son of David, the son of Abraham...*

God is Faithful – In Him I Trust

I come from a long lineage of Christians who laid the foundation for my faith! In Jesus I trust and am the recipient of His grace, favor, mercy, and faithfulness.

My attitude of gratitude today is for:

_____

_____

_____

_____

_____

_____

Chapter 2

Verses to Remember: 14-15

So he got up, took the child and His mother during the night and left for Egypt, where he stayed until the death of Herod. And so was fulfilled what the Lord had said through the prophet 'Out of Egypt I called my son.

Obedience is Worth its Weight in Gold

Lord, make me and mold me that I may hear your still small voice and heed your words as you direct me day by day. Joseph surely received your warning, brought by Your angel, in faith. He got up, took the child, and left.

My attitude of gratitude today is for:

_____

_____

_____

_____

_____

Chapter 3

Verses to Remember: 1-2

In those days John the Baptist came, preaching in the wilderness of Judea and saying, "Repent, for the kingdom of heaven has come near."

I'm a New Person in Jesus Christ

Because I have confessed my sins, repented, turned away from my old sinful ways, and accepted Jesus as my Savior, I share and look forward to eternity with my Creator. Praise be to God!

My attitude of gratitude today is for:

_____

_____

_____

_____

_____

Chapter 4

Verse to Remember: 16

The people living in darkness have seen a great light, on those living in the land of the shadow of death a light has dawned.

Jesus is Light!

Jesus' light shines wherever He resides. Lord, may Your light shine through my love and deeds for others. I honor you when I serve with love!

My attitude of gratitude today is for:

_____

_____

_____

_____

_____

_____

In the same way, let your light shine before others, that they may see your good deeds and glorify your Father in heaven.
Matthew 5:16

Chapter 5

Verse to Remember: 16

In the same way, let your light shine before others, that they may see your good deeds and glorify your Father in heaven.

Show the World the Difference Jesus Makes

Surrounded by needs, the Christian's role is to make a difference! Lord, may I see with Your eyes, hear with Your ears, touch with Your hands, feel with Your heart. When I do, I will be blessing someone!

My attitude of gratitude today is for:

_____

_____

_____

_____

_____

Chapter 6

Verse to Remember: 9

*After this manner therefore pray ye: Our Father which art
in heaven, Hallowed be thy name.*

My Father

Every day I need my Heavenly Father! I call on Him in
thought, in my heart, in my soul, using my mouth. I call on
Him because there is none like Him. I call on Him because He
is my everything – my refuge, my supply. He knows me and yet
loves me! The Lord's Prayer is the prayer that Jesus established
with His disciples for connection!

My attitude of gratitude today is for:

_____

_____

_____

_____

_____

Chapter 7

Verse to Remember: 7

> *Ask and it will be given to you, seek and you will find; knock and the door will be opened to you.*

Prayer in God's Will is Power

Lord, help me to pray and to seek Your will in my requests!

My attitude of gratitude today is for:

_____

_____

_____

_____

_____

_____

Do not store up for yourselves treasures on earth, where moth and rust destroy, and where thieves break in and steal.
Matthew 6:19

Chapter 8

Verse To Remember: 3

> *Jesus reached out his hand and touched the man. 'I am willing,' He said. 'Be clean!' Immediately, he was cleansed of his leprosy.*

Show Compassion

Jesus shows compassion as He restores us to Himself. His example must be my example – to reach out in love, care and concern to those in need. Lord, remove my blinders of busyness that I may not overlook those who are in need of my compassion.

My attitude of gratitude today is for:

_____

_____

_____

_____

_____

Chapter 9

Verse to Remember: 38

*Ask the Lord of the harvest, therefore, to send out workers
into his harvest field.*

Pray and Work

While I pray, I must also work toward that which I pray for.
God likes and blesses an action-packed faith. James would say
it this way – Faith without works is dead!

My attitude of gratitude today is for:

_____

_____

_____

_____

_____

_____

Chapter 10

Verse to Remember: 8

*Heal the sick, raise the dead, cleanse those who have leprosy,
drive out demons. Freely you have received, freely give.*

Serving Others in Need

Be given to serving those in need physically, mentally, and socially. This was God's instruction in addition to feeding them spiritually. I am surrounded by much need. Lord, open my eyes that I may see.

My attitude of gratitude today is for:

_____

_____

_____

_____

_____

Chapter 11

Verse to Remember: 28

Come to me, all you who are weary and burdened, and I will give you rest.

Strengthened by God on This Journey

Only through my connection to the Source of Power, my Heavenly Father, am I able to overcome the weariness that at times will come my way. Thank You Lord, for new mercies every day!

My attitude of gratitude today is for:

_____

_____

_____

_____

_____

Chapter 12

Verse to Remember: 18

Here is my servant whom I have chosen, the one I love, in whom I delight; I will put my Spirit on him, and he will proclaim justice to the nations.

Jesus Saves!

His descent from heaven was simply to save human kind. He left glory and perfection to come to a world made dark by my sins. Lord, thank You for such a great sacrifice. Help me day by day not to forget, but to live a life of gratitude, thanksgiving and hope in You.

My attitude of gratitude today is for:

_____

_____

_____

_____

_____

When the Son of Man comes in His glory, and all the angels with Him, He will sit on His glorious throne.
Matthew 25:31

Chapter 13

Verse to Remember: 44

The kingdom of heaven is like a treasure hidden in a field.
When a man found it, he hid it again, and then, in his joy, went
and sold all he had and bought the field.

Moving Toward Eternity with Jesus

Knowing Jesus and being His heir is one of the most important treasures I have. This treasure calls for total commitment! I will serve the Lord with everything I have!

My attitude of gratitude today is for:

_____

_____

_____

_____

_____

Chapter 14

Verse to Remember: 14

> *When Jesus landed and saw a large crowd, He had
> compassion on them and healed their sick.*

Jesus Has Compassion

Our lack is Jesus' opportunity to bless and to help. As He fed
more than 5,000 with 12 baskets still left, so He is willing to
feed us spiritually and physically. He desires to fill us so that
we may do His work in His kingdom.

My attitude of gratitude today is for:

_____

_____

_____

_____

_____

_____

Chapter 15

Verse to Remember: 3

And why do you break the command of God for the sake of your tradition?

Close To Thee

May I choose to draw closer to Thee Lord, rather than to impress those around me. Nothing should matter more than pleasing You by a closer walk with Thee. Lord, help me to do so!

My attitude of gratitude today is for:

_____

_____

_____

_____

_____

_____

But seek first His kingdom and His righteousness, and all these things will be given to you as well.
Matthew 6:33

Chapter 16

Verse to Remember: 21

*From that time on, Jesus began to explain to His disciples
that he must go to Jerusalem and suffer many things...*

Jesus is the Master Teacher

Lord, thank You for the daily lessons You teach me. A reluctant
student at times, I am getting better and better, as I learn the
important lessons about You and Who You are. It is glorious
to increase in knowledge of You.

My attitude of gratitude today is for:

_____

_____

_____

_____

_____

Chapter 17

Verse to Remember: 20

*He replied, "Because you have so little faith. Truly I tell you,
if you have faith as small as a mustard seed, you can say to
this mountain, 'Move from here to there,' and it will
move. Nothing will be impossible for you.*

It is a Journey of Faith

The journey of a believer is one of faith. It is trusting God for everything and anything, no matter what. Such faith requires drawing closer to Jesus Christ day by day. As I know Him personally as my Heavenly Father, I see His great love for me.

My attitude of gratitude today is for:

_____

_____

_____

_____

_____

Chapter 18

Verses To Remember: 21 -22

*Then Peter came to Jesus and asked, 'Lord, how many times
shall I forgive my brother or sister who sins against me? Up
to seven times?' Jesus answered, 'I tell you, not seven times,
but seventy-seven times.*

Reciprocate

God has, is, and will forgive my sins as I repent, confess, and
seek to walk closer to Him. Thank You Father for forgiveness
that wipes my slate clean!

Help me to look with compassion on my fellow human beings,
who, like me, have come short of the mark. Help me to
reciprocate what I have received from You, Lord.

My attitude of gratitude today is for:

_____

_____

_____

_____

_____

Chapter 19

Verse to Remember: 30

But many who are first will be last, and many who are last will be first.

God's Ways Are Not Our Ways

The least shall be first – losers will be winners. God's standards are supreme. His decisions are based on eternity, not the temporal. I am thankful that I serve an all-knowing God.

My attitude of gratitude today is for:

_____

_____

_____

_____

_____

Chapter 20

Verse to Remember: 23

Jesus said to them, 'You will indeed drink from my cup, but to sit at my right or left is not for me to grant. These places belong to those for whom they have been prepared by my Father.

Seek God's "Well Done" Only

The only affirmation that matters and is worth having is that which the Lord gives. Help me Lord, to remain focused on You as the reason for all that I do and not to seek the approval of mere men and women like me.

My attitude of gratitude today is for:

Ask and it will be given to you; seek and you will find; knock and the door will be opened to you.

Matthew 7:7

Chapter 21

Verse to Remember: 16

*Yes, have you never read, from the lips of children and infants
you, Lord, have called forth your praise.*

Praise God with a Childlike Heart

Children do what they do unabashedly and without
reservations - if it is running, jumping, climbing, singing, or
speaking. I must follow their example when praising my God.
He is worthy of my most uninhibited praise and adoration. He
is King of Kings and Lord of Lords.

My attitude of gratitude today is for:

_____

_____

_____

_____

Chapter 22

Verse to Remember: 39

And the second is like it: 'Love your neighbor as yourself.'

Love My Neighbor

God's commands are clear - to love Him with all of my heart, soul, and mind and to love my neighbor as myself. Lord, help me to exemplify Your love and concern for the needs all around me.

My attitude of gratitude today is for:

_____

_____

_____

_____

_____

Chapter 23

Verse To Remember: 37

*Jerusalem, Jerusalem, you who kill the prophets and stone
those sent to you, how often I have longed to gather you
children together, as a hen gathers her chicks under her wings,
and you were not willing.*

Jesus Cares

When Jesus' friend, Lazarus, died, scripture tells me that Jesus
wept. Just prior to His crucifixion, Jesus predicted with sadness
that the temple would be utterly destroyed because of Israel's
disobedience. Jesus' miraculous healing of the sick, the lame,
and the possessed are concrete examples of His caring about
the human condition. Lord, I thank you for love that cares and
reaches down to save and to help!

My attitude of gratitude today is for:

_____

_____

_____

Come unto me, all you who are weary and burdened, and I will give you rest.
Matthew 11:28

Chapter 24

Verse to Remember: 44

*Therefore be ye also ready: for in such an hour as ye think not
the Son of man cometh.*

Jesus' Return is Guaranteed!

Know that Jesus will return as He said He would! The
unknown factor is the time of His return. Therefore, live each
day in anticipation that it could be the day of His return. Lord,
may I be ready along with your remnant of loved ones.

My attitude of gratitude today is for:

_____

_____

_____

_____

_____

Chapter 25

Verses to Remember: 35-36

For I was hungry and you gave Me something to eat, I was thirsty and you gave Me something to drink, I was a stranger and you invited Me in, I needed clothes and you clothed Me, I was sick and you looked after Me, I was in prison and you came to visit Me.

Be Kind!

Kindness to fellow human beings is kindness to Jesus. When my heart is moved to meet the needs of others, I must exhibit the love that Jesus commanded that we show to each other. Lord, help me to see You in the faces of those in need.

My attitude of gratitude today is for:

_____

_____

_____

_____

_____

Chapter 26

Verse to Remember: 39

> *Going a little farther, He fell with His face to the ground and prayed, "My Father, if it is possible, may this cup be taken from me. Yet, not as I will, but as you will.*

Jesus Endured it All on Calvary

Jesus gave His life for me and endured rejection from His Father when He took on my sins. What a price to pay! Lord, help me never to take lightly Your great sacrifice. Because you did what You did, I have hope, joy, peace, and love in You.

My attitude of gratitude today is for:

_____

_____

_____

_____

_____

_____

Chapter 27

Verse to Remember: 50

*And when Jesus had cried out again in a loud voice,
He gave up His spirit.*

He Died For Me!

Calvary was by intention! It was a loving act for me! May I never lose sight of the great sacrifice made on my behalf by Jesus Christ. He reconciled me to God by His action. He took my sins upon Himself. He lives within my soul and walks with me each day. Thank You Lord!

My attitude of gratitude today is for:

_____

_____

_____

_____

_____

Chapter 28

Verse to Remember: 7

Then go quickly and tell His disciples…

Laundromat Day

Jesus commands that we go everywhere and tell His story that people might know Him and receive salvation. A story about ministry that started at the laundromat was a wonderful example of how Christians can reach others with the gospel of Jesus Christ in the least likely places. Jesus promised to be with us no matter where we go!

My attitude of gratitude today is for:

_____

_____

_____

_____

_____

When the Son of Man comes in his glory, and all the angels with Him, He
will sit on His glorious throne.
Matthew 25:31

35